MANCHESTER CITY

THE OFFICIAL ANNUAL 2020

C000000046

A Grange Publication

©2019 Published by Grange Communications Ltd., Edinburgh, under licence from Manchester City Football Club. Printed in the EU.

Edited by David Clayton
Designed by Simon Thorley
Photographs ©ManCity (Thanks to Victoria Haydn)

ISBN: 978-1-913034-24-5

CONTENTS

125 YEARS

FOURMIDABLES

THE STORY OF THE 2018/19 SEASON

AUGUST

Following a record-breaking season like the 2017/18 'Centurions' campaign was never going to be easy, but Pep Guardiola was determined to keep his players focused on trying to improve and be even better.

It was vital the Blues got off to a winning start and the FA Community Shield at Wembley offered the chance to start the season with a trophy. City took on FA Cup winners Chelsea and two Sergio Aguero goals were enough to win the game 2-0.

A week later, and a difficult trip to face Arsenal at the Emirates Stadium – never an easy venue and particularly as the Gunners had a new manager

in charge. But City made light work of the game, winning 2-0 with goals from Raheem Sterling and Bernardo Silva. The perfect start, and just a week later, the Blues sent out an ominous warning to the rest of the Premier League with a 6-1 win over Huddersfield Town – not a bad way to start your home campaign.

The goal of the game was when Ederson hit a 70-yard pass to the feet of Aguero who then turned and chipped the ball in off the underside of the bar from 20 yards. The month ended with a tricky 1-1 draw with newly-promoted Wolves and Aymeric Laporte's thumping header earned the champions a point.

Summary:
Played: 4 Won: 3
Drawn: 1 Lost: 0
Goals for: 11
Goals against: 2

SEPTEMBER

City had Kyle Walker to thank for starting September with a victory. A determined Newcastle United were holding City at the Etihad when Walker unleashed a powerful 25-yard shot to secure a vital 2-1 win. After brushing Fulham aside 3-0 following an international break, City then embarked on their Champions League campaign, but Lyon shocked the Etihad crowd by going 2-0 up at half-time – Bernardo pulled one back but the Blues lost 2-1 to the French side, making the group stage even tougher.

Three days later and normal service was resumed as City travelled to South Wales and thrashed Cardiff 5-0. Three goals in 12 minutes before the break put the Blues in total command and two Riyad Mahrez strikes in the second half completed the rout. And the goals kept flowing with a 3-0 Carabao Cup win away to Oxford a few days later – a game in which Phil Foden scored his first senior goal. The month ended with a 2-0 win over Brighton and put City back at the top of the table as Liverpool dropped their first points.

Summary:
Played: 5 Won: 4
Drawn: 0 Lost: 1
Goals for: 16 Goals
against: 3

OCTOBER

City bounced back from the Champions League loss to Lyon by winning the next game against Hoffenheim, though it was far from straightforward after going behind in the first minute! In fact, City were still 1-0 down until Aguero levelled on 72 minutes and three minutes from time, David Silva struck the winner.

Next up, the toughest test so far – Liverpool away. In a tense and measured game, City were handed the chance of a first win at Anfield in 15 years when Leroy Sane was fouled in the box, but Mahrez hit his penalty high over the bar and the Blues had to settle for a 0-0 draw.

A week later and the goals were flowing again as former keeper Joe Hart saw five goals put past him as City beat Burnley 5-0 at the Etihad. A 3-0 Champions League win away to Shakhtar Donetsk followed and an early goal from Mahrez at Wembley secured a vital 1-0 win over Tottenham to keep City top of the Premier League, going into the winter months.

Summary:
Played: 5 Won: 4
Drawn: 1 Lost: 0
Goals for: 11
Goals against: 1

NOVEMBER

November started well for City with a 2-0 Carabao Cup win over Fulham followed by a thumping Premier League win over Southampton. The Blues raced into a 4-1 lead at the break, going on to win 6-1. A Wesley Hoedt own goal plus strikes from David Silva, Aguero, Sterling (2) and Sane did the damage and as a result, the Blues moved two points clear of second-placed Chelsea and Liverpool.

Three days later and the Blues again hit six, with a 6-0 win over Shakhtar Donetsk at the Etihad – the goals were flowing thick and fast, and City went into the Manchester derby full of confidence with goals from Aguero and Ilkay Gundogan (2) seeing off Jose Mourinho's side 3-1 at the Etihad.

The rampant Blues then thrashed West Ham at the London Stadium, racing into a three-goal lead with just 34 minutes played before going on to add another after half-time in a comfortable 4-0 win.

Tottenham were hanging in there in third spot, just five points off the top spot but Chelsea were starting to fall away somewhat. For neutrals, however, the title race was all about the battle between City and Liverpool - two teams, focused, defensively strong and blessed with free-scoring attacks going neck and neck for the ultimate prize in domestic football.

Summary:
Played: 5 Won: 5
Drawn: 0 Lost: 0
Goals for: 21
Goals against: 2

The Blues kicked off December with a fairly straightforward 3-1 win over Bournemouth with Bernardo, Sterling and Gundogan all on target. City next endured a tricky end to what had otherwise been a comfortable midweek visit to Watford, clinging on to win 2-1 after a late onslaught from the Hornets.

As Christmas approached, the Blues – still in all four competitions – had their first real setback of the season at Stamford Bridge, where City fell behind on the stroke of half-time to Ngolo Kante's thunderous goal. Chelsea added a second late on to secure a 2-0 win and end the Blues' unbeaten start to the season and also end a 21-game unbeaten Premier League run. Liverpool seized the initiative with a 4-0 win at Bournemouth to go top, but things were about to get worse for the champions.

The next game City beat Everton 3-1 at the Etihad and then beat Hoffenheim 2-1 in the Champions League. The Blues also progressed to the semi-final of the Carabao Cup after beating Leicester 3-1 on penalties before hosting struggling Crystal Palace. When Gundogan's header on 27 minutes put the Blues ahead, there seemed little doubt City would go on and win comfortably. However, just eight minutes later, Palace had turned the game on its head and were 2-1 up - the second goal

an absolute stunner from Andros Townsend, who volleyed an unstoppable shot from more than 30 yards out. Worse was to come as the lively Palace belied their lowly position with a third from the penalty spot on 52 minutes following a clumsy Kyle Walker challenge. Kevin De Bruyne, absent for most of the campaign with a knee injury, pulled a late goal back but Palace held on to a deserved 3-2 win.

An instant response was needed and the Boxing Day trip to Leicester provided the opportunity to do exactly that. The Blues took the initiative at the King Power with Bernardo Silva's 14th-minute strike, but the Foxes, sensing apprehension from City, soon levelled and Ricardo Pereira's late winner completed a miserable festive period for the champions who now trailed Liverpool by seven points.

City knew another slip would probably end hopes of retaining the Premier League title – even with half the campaign still to go - and so headed to Southampton needing to end the year with nothing less than a victory. Pep Guardiola was confident his team would deliver and put what had been a severe hiccup behind them – and by the break City were proving him right, leading Saints 3-1, even if the display hadn't been vintage City.

Summary:
Played: 9 Won: 6
Drawn: 0 Lost: 3
Goals for: 16
Goals against: 12

There were tension, nerves and anxiety in the air as City and Liverpool walked out at the Etihad for their latest titanic tussle – what a way to start the New Year! It wasn't winner takes all, but it felt like the result of this encounter would have a huge bearing on the title race. For the Blues, a victory would not only end the Merseysiders' unbeaten start, it would reduce the gap to the leaders to just four – a loss for City would see a surely insurmountable 10-point advantage for Klopp's side with only 17 games remaining.

In a blood and thunder contest, Liverpool almost went ahead when Sadio Mane's scuffed effort hit the post. The ball was cleared against Ederson and was rolling towards the empty net when John Stones somehow hooked his foot around it to clear the danger. The goal-line technology suggested the ball had been a couple of millimetres short of being given as a goal and City survived. The first goal would be crucial, and it was City who broke the deadlock when Aguero fired a powerful angled shot past Allison just before the break, to send the Etihad crazy.

The contest, however, was far from over and after a spell of sustained pressure, Roberto Firmino levelled on 64 minutes to keep the match finely balanced. It felt like Liverpool suddenly had the momentum, but City dug deep, stood strong and on 79 minutes, Leroy Sane's low shot beat Allison and went in off the post to once again send the Etihad wild and the Blues held out to win 2-1.

City followed the victory by going goal crazy. First up, Rotherham were beaten 7-0 in the FA Cup third round and then the Blues thrashed League One side Burton Albion 9-0 in the first leg of the Carabao Cup semi-final. Successive 3-0 wins over Wolves and Huddersfield followed in the League before further cup victories over Burton (1-0) and Burnley (5-0) in the Carabao Cup and FA Cup respectively. The last game of the month was away to Newcastle United. City could hardly have started better on Tyneside, taking the lead after just 24 seconds through Aguero, but the failure to capitalise on that flying start allowed the Magpies' belief to grow.

When Solomon Rondon levelled on 66 minutes, the doubt that had surfaced around Christmas seemed to re-emerge and when Fernandinho's challenge resulted in a late penalty, converted by Matt Ritchie, it gave the Magpies a 2-1 win and ended a long losing streak against the champions. After working so hard to get back in the title race, had the Blues now shot themselves in the foot? As it was, Leicester managed a surprise draw away to Liverpool a day later and while Jurgen Klopp's side were five points clear, it should have been seven. The race was still on.

Summary:
Played: 8 Won: 7
Drawn: 0 Lost: 1
Goals for: 30
Goals against: 3

FEBRUARY

City roared into February on top form, starting the month with a 3-1 win over Arsenal, courtesy of yet another Aguero hat-trick. A tricky 2-0 win at Everton was backed up by a mesmerising 6-0 win over Chelsea, as the champions exacted revenge on the West London side who had ended the Blues' unbeaten start – and Aguero bagged yet another treble!

And City – already Carabao Cup finalists – moved into the quarter-finals of the FA Cup with a 4-1 win over League Two minnows Newport County. The goals just kept flowing! 10-man City then beat Schalke 3-2 in the Champions League Round of 16 first leg in Germany before securing the second piece of silverware of the season against Chelsea.

The teams met in the Carabao Cup final at Wembley and after a 0-0 draw, City won the penalty shoot-out 4-3 to win the trophy. And Aguero's 59th-minute penalty against West Ham ended February with three more vital points to leave the Blues just one behind leaders Liverpool with 10 games to go.

MARCH

City's rich vein of form would continue during March with people starting to wonder whether the Blues could be the first English men's team to win the quadruple. A narrow 1-0 win at Bournemouth was followed by a 3-1 win at home to Watford and a 13-minute hat-trick from Sterling.

The Blues dismantled Schalke in the return Champions League leg with seven unanswered goals at the Etihad, completing a 10-2 aggregate win. A trip to Championship side Swansea in the FA Cup quarter-final was less comfortable and the Blues found themselves 2-0 down with only 20 minutes remaining – but goals from Bernardo, an own goal by the keeper and a last-minute diving header from Aguero secured a dramatic 3-2 victory.

The Blues ended March with a 2-0 win at Fulham to move one point clear of Liverpool with just seven games remaining.

Summary:
Played: 5 Won: 5
Drawn: 0 Lost: 0
Goals for: 16
Goals against: 3

Summary:
Played: 7 Won: 7
Drawn: 0 Lost: 0
Goals for: 19
Goals against: 4

Summary:
Played: 8 Won: 7
Drawn: 0 Lost: 1
Goals for: 14
Goals against: 5

APRIL

April would be yet another breathless month full of goals, thrills and drama.

City began by easing past Cardiff 2-0 at the Etihad before heading off to Wembley in the FA Cup semi-final. Gabriel Jesus' early diving header was enough to beat Brighton 1-0 and book an FA Cup final spot for the first time since 2013 where Watford awaited.

City's Champions League hopes took a blow with a 1-0 first leg loss to Spurs in the quarter-final clash at the north London side's state-of-the-art new stadium. Things would have been different had Sergio Aguero converted an early penalty, but the Blues knew they were more than capable of turning the tie around.
Before the second leg, City gained revenge on Crystal Palace for the defeat at the Etihad in December, running out comfortable 3-1 winners at Selhurst Park.

Then – one of the most dramatic nights the Etihad Stadium had ever witnessed as City hosted Spurs in the Champions League quarter-final second leg. What a game! City took an early lead through Sterling, but two quick goals from Son Heung-min put Spurs in the driving seat – until Bernardo levelled almost straight away. It was 2-2 with only 12 minutes played! City went

ahead before the break, and when Aguero made it 4-2 just before the hour mark, the Blues were finally ahead in the tie.

But Fernando Llorente's controversial 73rd-minute goal was allowed to stand despite striking his arm and the referee taking several looks at the incident on VAR. And it looked as though City were going out with just seconds remaining until Aguero raced into the box and squared the ball to Sterling to score. The City fans, players and even Pep went crazy – until the words 'VAR review' were flashed on the scoreboard. Incredibly, the goal was disallowed, and City were out, but what a game of football.

The teams met for the third time in nine days the following Saturday with Phil Foden's header enough to win a tense game 1-0.
A tired looking City knew that if they won the games that remained, they would be champions, but there were still some hard games to come. First up, the Blues had to go to Old Trafford in the Manchester derby and after a goalless first half, goals from Bernardo and Sane swung the game City's way and a vital 2-0 victory. The Blues, not at their best, had done enough and next travelled to Burnley where Aguero's shot was judged to have crossed the lines by millimetres to secure a priceless 1-0 win at Turf Moor.

A thrilling title race with Liverpool would soon be over, but who would end up being champions? With just two games remaining, City hosted Leicester knowing just six more points would mean the title was won. But few could have predicted the night of drama at the Etihad with Leicester looking dangerous and revitalised under new manager Brendan Rodgers and with 70 minutes gone, the score was still 0-0. Then, skipper Vincent Kompany picked up the ball and shaped to take a shot – as everybody urged him not to, the Belgian unleashed a shot into the top right-hand corner from 25 yards out to give City all three points. Incredible stuff.

That meant a win at Brighton on the final day and City would be champions. Brighton, safe from relegation, surely couldn't stop the Blues winning back-to-back titles? But when Glenn Murray headed the home side ahead, Liverpool – beating Wolves at Anfield – were suddenly two points clear in the live league table. But City responded immediately with Aguero grabbing his 32nd goal of the season just a minute later and then Laporte headed City in front before the break. The celebrations began when Mahrez scored a beauty just past the hour-mark and Gundogan's stunning free-kick on 72 minutes sealed a 4-1 win – and the Premier League title. City finished on 98 points with Liverpool on 97, ending one of the most thrilling campaigns in Premier League history.

But there was still one game to play and City could still complete a domestic clean sweep of all four English trophies against Watford at Wembley in the FA Cup final. And what a day it proved to be, with City at their majestic best, sweeping the Hornets aside 6-0 with two goals for Gabriel Jesus and Raheem Sterling plus further strikes from David Silva and Kevin De Bruyne.

It was a fitting end to end a quite incredible season.

Summary:
Played: 3 Won: 3
Drawn: 0 Lost: 0
Goals for: 11
Goals against: 1

GUESS WHO? #1

Can you figure out who these City players are? We've disguised four images to hide their true identities – but can you use your detective skills to work out who they are?

01

02

03

04

Answers on page 60&61

WORDSEARCH#1

There are 10 City players' names in the wordsearch below – horizontal and vertical... see how many you can find!

```
L O Z Y K L N N K T N P
M D I D D K K T K O G A
D R N F K N R Z S G I J
R A C W O D E R M C Z L
M N H A K D E M R J A R
T R E L L D E A R P H T
J E N K E L G N O L S C
N B K E V W F R R V E B
F N O R P P T J F B N K
R K G G K E G L Q K O Q
N S T E R L I N G M T F
V Z E R H A M T B C S G
```

STONES

WALKER

BERNARDO

EDERSON

ZINCHENKO

MENDY

STERLING

LAPORTE

GARCIA

FODEN

MAHREZ

15

Answers on page 60&61

2019/20 SUMMER SIGNING#1:
RODRI

Rodrigo Hernández Cascante, better known as 'Rodri', joined City on 4 July 2019 after agreeing a five-year contract. The 23-year-old Spanish midfielder joined from Atletico Madrid and became Pep Guardiola's second signing of the summer.

The defensively-minded midfielder is most at home sitting in front of the back four, where Rodri has earned a reputation as one of Europe's most exciting prospects. He will wear the number 16 shirt for City.

Born on 23 June 1996, Rodri supported Atleti as a boy.

He joined Atletico Madrid's youth set-up in 2007 aged 11, from CF Rayo Majadahonda and progressed through their academy ranks before departing in 2013 to complete his youth development at Villarreal. One of their most coveted prospects, Rodri made his debut in December 2015 aged 19 and went on to represent the Yellow Submarine 84 times in three seasons.

Combining an impressive reading of the game with great touch, Rodri won admirers for his ability to break up opposition attacks before setting up his own with his thoughtful range of passing.

After making 64 La Liga appearances for Villarreal, Rodri returned to Atletico Madrid in May 2018 for a fee in the region of £20million. During a hugely impressive 2018/19 La Liga campaign, he made 34 appearances for Atletico, scoring three goals and it was

at Wanda Metropolitano where he further enhanced his reputation.

Standing at 6"3' and with his technical ability and tactical understanding of the game both equally impressive, Rodri has been compared to Sergio Busquets. He is studying for a degree and while in Spain, was happy driving a small, second-hand car rather than anything expensive! He also has no social media presence – again unusual for a modern footballer and is fluent in English.

He helped Atleti lift the 2018 UEFA Super Cup with a 4-2 victory over Real Madrid and went on to play 47 times, scoring three goals as his home-town club finished second in La Liga.

After representing Spain at Under-16 and Under-19, he was part of the U19 squad which won the 2015 European Championships, where he was named in the team of the tournament. He also won caps at Under-21 level before being called into the full Spain squad for the first time in March 2018 ahead of two friendlies with Germany and Argentina.

He has won six caps for Spain and is expected to be the long-term successor to the brilliant Fernandinho.

RODRI: *FACTFILE*

No.16: Rodri

Date of birth: 23/6/96

Birthplace: Madrid, Spain

Nationality: Spanish

Position: Defensive midfield

CROSSWORD

Can you solve the Manchester City crossword puzzle by working out the clues across and down?

ACROSS

1 One of our mascots!
5 French full-back formerly with Monaco
10 Name given to City's players after winning all four domestic trophies
14 He was voted PFA Young Player of the Year
15 Our brilliant Brazilian goalkeeper
17 With 32 goals, he was City's top scorer in 2018/19
18 City's Etihad Player of the Year for 2018/19
19 He's known as 'El Mago' - The Magician
20 City captain who left for Anderlecht

DOWN

2 Nickname for City
3 Belgian playmaker
4 City and England right-back
6 Our Brazilian anchor-man
7 City Women and England goalkeeper
8 City Women's captain
9 Goalkeeper who once captained Chile
11 Fan song most associated with City
12 German winger, formerly with Schalke
13 City play their home games here
16 Algerian star who joined from Leicester

Answers on page 60&61

SPOT THE BALL#1

Can you spot the ball? We've removed the real ball from the picture below, so you'll have to use detective work to try and figure out exactly which grid it's in – it's tricky and maybe not as obvious as it first looks – the players' faces may offer a few clues... or do they?

Answers on page 60&61

EDERSON

THE ULTIMATE KEEPER

125 YEARS

Here are 10 facts you didn't know about a goalkeeper we reckon is the best in the world...

1. In May 2018, City invited a Guinness Book of World Records adjudicator to the City Football Academy so Ederson could attempt to break the current record of 75 metres for the longest drop kick. After two attempts fell just short, Ederson launched his third attempt an incredible 75.35 metres to set a new world record. So, not only is he the best 'keeper in the world, he also holds the world record to prove it!

2. His full name is Ederson Santana de Moraes and he was born on 17 August 1993 in Osasco, Brazil.

3. His nickname in Brazil was 'The Bull' because of the way he charged out of his box towards strikers.

4. Ederson has scored goals, of course! As a youth in Brazil, he once scored from his own box with a huge kick up field.

5. Ederson played alongside – and eventually replaced Brazilian legend Julio Cesar at Benfica – one of Brazil's greatest 'keepers and somebody who helped Ederson develop his trade.

6. Ederson has more than 30 tattoos on his body with each one having a meaning in his life or family. Some are religious but others, such as the smiley face behind his ear, are just for fun and reflect his easy-going nature.

7. Ederson grew up idolising Rogério Ceni, the former Brazil international who is the top-scoring goalkeeper of all-time with 131 goals in his 25-year career at São Paulo! Ederson once said of Ceni: "He is my only idol and will always be my main inspiration. I still watch many of his videos making amazing saves and showing his quality to start his team's play from the back. His quality was extraordinary."

8. Ederson was born in Osasco, a tough neighbourhood in São Paulo and it won't be a surprise to learn he started out life as a left-back at a football school called Champions Ebenézer FC. Though the coach was impressed with the power of his shots, he couldn't dribble well enough and so he put him in goal instead. The rest is history!

9. Ederson celebrated his 100th appearance for City by making a crucial save at 0-0 in the 2019 FA Cup final after which the Blues went on to win 6-0.

10. After just two years at City, he had become the Club's most decorated goalkeeper in history, winning two Premier League titles, two Carabao Cups, one FA Cup and one FA Community Shield. He was also voted in the PFA Team of the Year 2018/19.

MAN CITY WOMEN

2018/19 SEASON REVIEW

It was another fantastic season for Manchester City Women who continue to be a powerful force in English football. Led by coach Nick Cushing, City started the season as one of the favourites for the FA Women's Super League title.

Captained by the brilliant Steph Houghton, City had quality throughout the team, from goalkeeper Karen Bardsley, through to striker Nikita Parris and began the season well, with the only disappointment being knocked out of the UEFA Women's Champions League at the first hurdle.

City would be locked in a title battle with Arsenal all season and it appeared the season may be decided on the final day with City away to Arsenal. But crucial dropped points

against Chelsea at the Academy Stadium meant Arsenal won the title with a game to spare.

City had been unbeaten all season in the league but lost to a last-minute goal to Arsenal on the final day – virtually the last kick of the season – but the Gunners were already champions after an epic title battle.
But the Blues were not ending the season empty-handed – far from it!

Steph Houghton had already lifted the Continental Cup (on the same weekend City's men team won the Carabao Cup against Chelsea) after a penalty shootout win over… you guessed it – Arsenal.

With one piece of silverware already won, City then made it all the way to Wembley where West Ham United awaited in the Women's FA Cup final. Watched by a crowd of more than 43,000, City beat the Hammers 3-0 to win the trophy for only the second time.

So, while the league title went to Arsenal, City won both domestic cup competitions to complete a terrific campaign. Nikita Parris scored 22 goals in 25 games to finish top scorer, earning her the coveted Football Writers' Association Women's Player of the Year, though she would join Olympique Lyon shortly after.

City's target in 2019/20 is to, again, challenge for the title and domestic cups as well as aim for Champions League progression.
You can watch all Manchester City Women's home games at the Academy Stadium.
Check www.mancity.com for the latest fixture information and get down and cheer the girls on!

2019/20 SUMMER SIGNING#2:

JOSE 'ANGELINO' ESMORIS TASENDE

Angelino was born Jose Angel Esmoris Tasende on 4 January 1997 in the small Spanish town of Coristanco.

At the age of 10, Angelino joined Deportivo La Coruna's youth set-up. During his six years with Deportivo, Angelino was continually linked with Barcelona and Real Madrid, showing just how highly rated the youngster was.

In January 2013, Angelino joined Manchester City's Academy where he made a big impression at both Under-18 and Under-23 level, going on to win the MCFC EDS Player of the Year in his first full campaign.

Three years later, Angelino made his first team debut at the age of 19 in an FA Cup match against Aston Villa, coming on for Gael Clichy at 81 minutes as City went on to win 4-0.

He then featured as a substitute in City's 1-0 Champions League victory over Steaua Bucharest in August of that year before making his first start in a 2-1 League Cup success over Swansea City.

To further aid his development and experience Angelino then enjoyed four loan spells around the world – in America with New York City FC; in Spain with Girona and Majorca; and in Holland with NAC Breda during the 2017/18 campaign where he won the Rookie of the Month award four times.

This was followed by his move to PSV Eindhoven in August of last year where Angelino enjoyed a stellar campaign in the Eredivisie. Angelino played 34 league appearances for PSV, scoring one goal and providing 10 assists. He also impressed for PSV in the Champions League, playing in all six of their group games against Barcelona, Spurs and Inter Milan. In both Angelino's seasons at PSV he was voted onto the Eredivisie Team of the Year.

Now the 22-year-old defender has sealed his return to Manchester City having signed a four-year contract which will keep him at the club until the summer of 2023.

ANGELINO: *FACTFILE*

No.12: Angelino
Date of birth: 04/01/1997
Birthplace: Coristanco, Spain
Nationality: Spanish
Position: Attacking left-back

THE BIG CITY QUIZ 2020...

40 questions to test your City knowledge to the max! There's 100 points available – can you become a Fourmidable – or will you settle for a Champions League spot? All questions are based on last season...

01

City had two players sent off during 2018/19 – can you name them both?

02

Which club did Vincent Kompany leave City to player-manage?

03

Who were the only Premier League side to beat City at home in 2018/19?

04

Who scored a 13-minute hat-trick against Watford?

05

Who scored both City goals in the 2-0 2018 FA Community Shield win against Chelsea?

06

Which Welsh League 2 club side did City beat in the FA Cup?

*Clue

26

07

True or false? City had two VAR decisions go against them in the Champions League home tie with Tottenham.

08

Who did Phil Foden score his first Premier League goal against?

09

Which country does goalkeeper Aro Muric represent?

10

Danilo scored one goal in 2018/19 – who was it against?

11

Who was voted the Football Writers' Player of the Year?

12

How many German teams did City face in the 2018/19 Champions League?

*Clue

13

Who missed a penalty away to Liverpool?

14

Who scored five headers – all away from home?

*Clue

15

What aggregate score did City record against Burton Albion? A) 9-1 B) 10-0 C) 11-0

16

Where was Bernardo born? A) Lisbon B) Porto C) Braga

17

Who wears the No.31 shirt for City?

18
Which French team beat City at the Etihad in the Champions League?

19
How many times has David Silva won the Premier League?

20
How many times did City play at Wembley in 2018/19? A) 3 B) 4 C) 5

21
Which team did City beat 5-0 twice at the Etihad?

22
Who scored City's 100th home goal of the season?

23
Who scored in City's last game of 2018 and first game of 2019?

24
In the Carabao Cup final penalty shoot-out against Chelsea, who was the only City player to miss?

25
Who did City play in the FA Youth Cup final?

26
How many trophies did Manchester City Women win?

27
City beat Chelsea in the Carabao Cup penalty shoot-out – by what score?

28
Who else did City beat on penalties in the Carabao Cup?

*Clue

29
How many Premier League games did City win at the Etihad in 2018/19?

30
City played 10 games in London in all competitions – how many ended in victory?

31

Which of these three clubs did City NOT beat home and away? A) Manchester United B) Newcastle United C) Everton

32

Who left City for Barcelona?

*Clue

33

Who did Oleksandr Zinchenko score his only goal of the season against?

34

True or false? City scored in all 28 home games (all competitions) in 2018/19.

35

True or false? City played their first and last games of the 2018/19 season at Wembley.

36

Who was the only City player to take part in the Africa Cup of Nations 2019?

37

City signed a new kit deal with which company?

38

Which shirt number does Kevin De Bruyne wear?

*Clue

39

Which Canary Island is David Silva from? A) Tenerife B) Lanzarote C) Gran Canaria

40

Which of these teams did Pep Guardiola NOT play for? A) Espanyol B) Roma C) Barcelona

Answers on page 60-61

SPOT THE BALL #2

Here we go again! We've removed the real ball from the picture below - the Manchester derby at Old Trafford on this occasion - so you'll have to use detective work to try and figure out exactly which grid it is in. Leroy has fired in a shot – but where is the ball heading? Good luck!

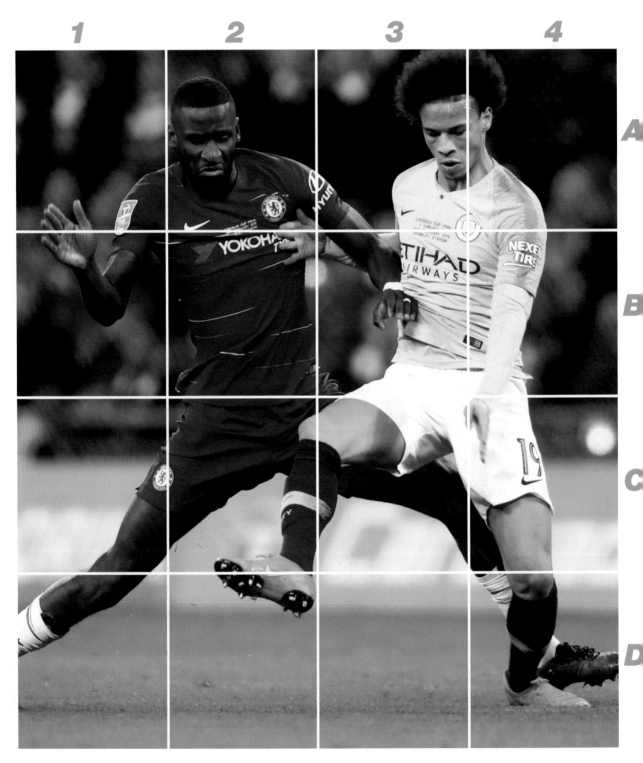

Answers on page 60&61

GUESS WHO? #2

Here are four mystery City players – use your powers of observation and detective work to discover their identities

01

02

03

04

ELLEN WHITE

Manchester City 125 YEARS

125 YEARS

2019/20 SUMMER SIGNING#3:
JOAO CANCELO

"Versatile attacking full-back…"

Highly-rated Portuguese right-back Joao Cancelo joined City from Juventus in August 2019 after several months of rumoured interest from the Blues.
The defender penned a six-year deal which keeps him at the Etihad Stadium until the summer of 2025 and after the arrivals of Angelino and Rodrigo, became Pep Guardiola's third signing of the summer.

During his season with Juventus, Cancelo established himself as one of Serie A's best full-backs. Comfortable on either flank and capable of playing in a more advanced position, Cancelo provides great delivery from wide areas and boasts exceptional athleticism, using his pace to good effect in both offensive and defensive situations.

Technically, the Portuguese is excellent, and he is an exciting player the City fans will enjoy watching, particularly when he is going forward or racing down the flanks to support attacks. His occasional trickery on the ball and accuracy when delivering crosses into the box will fit well into Pep Guardiola's attacking philosophy.

Cancelo's professional career began with Benfica, where he progressed through their academy and won the 2013 Portuguese U19 Championship alongside future City star Bernardo Silva.

He made his senior debut the following season, when the Lisbon giants claimed a domestic treble, but joined Valencia on a year-long loan in 2014/15 and did enough in 13 games to convince Los Che to make the deal permanent.

He went on to play 77 times over the next two campaigns before heading off on loan again, this time to Inter Milan, where he again thrived in a new environment.

Cancelo's form convinced Juventus to make him one of their major signings for 2018/19 campaign, where he teamed up with international team-mate Cristiano Ronaldo and he again impressed in Turin, winning praise for his committed attacking play which yielded one goal and five assists in 34 games as Juventus lifted an eighth successive Serie A title.

He followed that up with his first taste of international success, winning the inaugural UEFA Nations League title with Portugal this summer and by the start of the 2019/20 season, he had won 16 full caps and represented his country through various age levels (Under-16s, 17s, 18s, 19s, 20s and 21s) 89 times in total.

Brazilian full-back Danilo joined Juventus as part of the deal.

CANCELO: *FACTFILE*

No.27: Joao Cancelo

Date of birth: 27 May 1994

Location: Barreiro, Portugal

Nationality: Portuguese

Position: Right-back

Joined City: 7 August 2019

BERNARDO:
ETIHAD PLAYER OF THE YEAR

Bernardo Silva was the runaway winner when Manchester City fans voted for their player of the season.

The Portuguese playmaker became a huge crowd favourite during the 2018/19 season during which he shone throughout. Bernardo may be slight in physical build, but the diminutive attacking midfielder has a huge heart, is brave and plays with passion and energy.

There were many times during the Fourmidables season that he upped his game to even higher levels when the team needed to win the most, and his stunning performance in the 2-1 win over Liverpool proved just how vital he is to City as he chased every ball, covered every blade of grass and ensured Liverpool's defenders were never allowed to settle.

But that was just one example of this gifted footballer's contribution. He began the season with a stunning goal in the 2-0 win at Arsenal and never looked back from there. He created goals, scored vital goals and displayed exceptional skill with some fantastic dribbles. When he was at Benfica, his nickname was 'Bubblegum' because people used to say the ball would stick to his foot.

Away from the pitch, he is a hugely popular guy with his team-mates and the Club's staff and the fans continually singing his name throughout the season, even creating a new chant based on an old Abba song, 'Voulez Vous'!

It's no wonder manager Pep Guardiola said, "As long as I am at City, Bernardo will be a Manchester City player." Let's hope they are both around for a long, long time!

BERNARDO SILVA: *FACTFILE*

Name: Bernardo Mota Veiga de Carvalho e Silva

Born: 10 August 1994

Birthplace: Lisbon, Portugal

Former clubs: Benfica B, Benfica, Monaco

Career games: 287

Career goals: 57

International caps: 38

International goals: 3

Manchester City appearances: 100

Manchester City goals: 22

*all stats corrects as of 1 August 2019

OUR PORTUGUESE CROWD FAVOURITE...

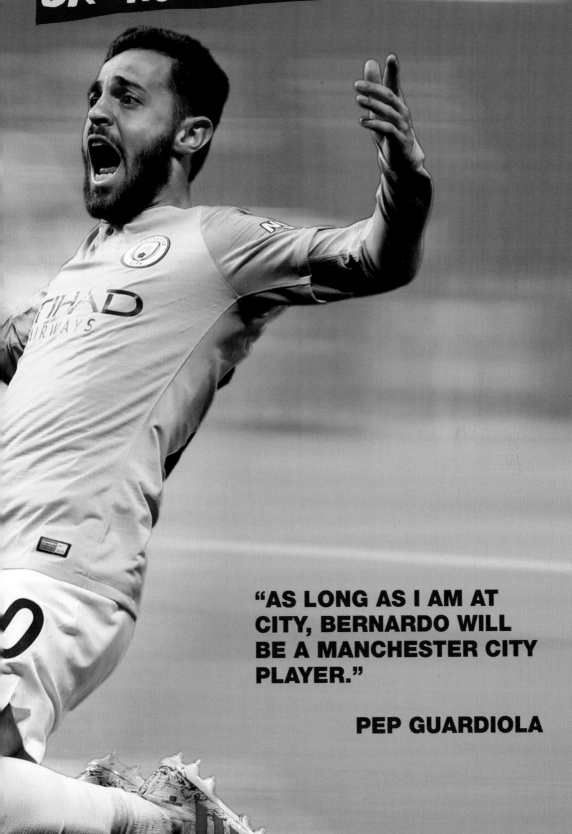

"AS LONG AS I AM AT CITY, BERNARDO WILL BE A MANCHESTER CITY PLAYER."

PEP GUARDIOLA

COUNTDOWN
TO KICK-OFF

What happens on the run-up to a match at the Etihad Stadium as the clock ticks towards kick-off..? Based on a 3pm Saturday home game, here is the matchday routine of the City players and the backroom coaching staff...

11AM

City's Kit Manager and his assistants James and Brandon arrive at the Etihad to unload and prepare the kit, based on the team-sheet for the day. Shirts, shorts and socks will be laid on the tables next to the players' seats, and boots will be placed in readiness for the team arrival. Warm-up shirts will also be provided.

12PM

The team enjoy a light lunch at the CFA player canteen before preparing for their departure over to the Etihad Stadium.

1PM

The turnstiles at the Etihad Stadium open to allow fans access to the concourses and stadium bowl.

1.15PM

Team meeting with Pep Guardiola to go over key points and tactical fine-tuning.

1.38PM

The team coach makes the short journey to the Etihad Stadium.

1.45PM

Arrival at the Etihad where players alight and are introduced as they step off the coach and head for the changing rooms.

2.15PM

The goalkeepers are usually first out for a warm-up on the Etihad pitch with the rest of the team joining a light warm-up session which will include gentle sprints, stretches, keep-ball sessions and shooting. The substitutes will generally warm-up separately.

2.45PM

The players return from their warm-up to get ready for the game. This will mean putting their match kit on, possibly change their boots and add whatever extras they need in terms of strappings or anything else needed.

2.50PM

Pep Guardiola will deliver his final team talk and emphasise any tactical instructions/observations on the opposition.

2.55PM

Both sets of players walk out and line-up before City are led by the captain along the line of opposition players where handshakes are exchanged. The City players run towards the North Stand to stretch their legs before handing tracksuit tops to the kit man in readiness for kick-off.

3.00PM

Preparation over – match begins!

3.45PM

(approx.): Half-time – time for refreshments, energy bars and fruit as well as Pep Guardiola's observations of the first half – what is working well and where the players can improve.

4.55PM

(approx.) Match ends – the stadium begins to empty while the players leave the pitch. One or two players will be asked to do immediate TV media as will the manager who, after briefly talking to the players in the changing room, will then head off for the press conference.

WORDSEARCH#2

There are 10 City players' names in the wordsearch below – horizontal, vertical and diagonal… see how many you can find!

```
C  G  J  L  C  B  Z  Z  X  H  N
L  I  T  E  D  E  L  P  H  R  A
O  F  R  R  S  Y  M  K  H  D  G
T  P  T  U  D  U  A  B  A  X  O
A  T  D  K  M  I  S  G  K  W  D
M  D  R  G  C  K  U  M  A  O  N
E  K  N  R  M  E  X  V  M  V  U
N  K  A  X  R  T  L  M  B  A  G
D  G  C  O  J  I  P  F  Y  R  F
I  L  C  F  S  F  H  T  B  B  M
O  H  N  I  D  N  A  N  R  E  F
```

GUNDOGAN	**AGUERO**
SILVA	**FERNANDINHO**
DELPH	**MURIC**
JESUS	**BRAVO**
OTAMENDI	**GARCIA**

Answers on page 60&61

PHIL FODEN:

11 THINGS YOU DIDN'T KNOW!

Our brilliant teenage midfielder is one of English football's brightest talents – but do you know everything there is to know about this precocious talent..?

1. Phil, from Stockport near Manchester, is a lifelong Manchester City supporter and comes from a long line of City supporters.

2. Phil was once an Etihad ball boy for City's first team.

3. One of Phil's favourite hobbies is late night fishing with his dad, Phil Senior.

4. Phil was awarded the FIFA Under-17 Golden Ball – the honour given to the tournament's most valuable player - as England Under-17s went on to win the U17s World Cup.

5. Phil has earned the nickname 'The Stockport Iniesta' by some of the Club's coaching staff, comparing the teenager to Barcelona legend Andres Iniesta.

6. Phil began his football journey with local Stockport junior team Reddish Vulcans – and it was with them he was spotted by Manchester City scout Joe Makin.

7. Even up to the age of 16 and after he had been with City since the age of nine, Phil used to go and help coach at Reddish Vulcans on a Saturday morning.

8. One of Phil's mentors at City is also one of his heroes – David Silva.

9. Phil realised a boyhood dream when he scored his first Premier League goal at the Etihad – a diving header that gave City a crucial 1-0 win over Tottenham on the way to a second successive Premier League title.

10. Phil was the youngest recipient of a Premier League winner's medal.

11. In 2017, he was awarded the BBC Young Personality of the Year.

2019/20 COMMUNITY SHIELD WINNERS!

The champions start as they mean to go on...

44

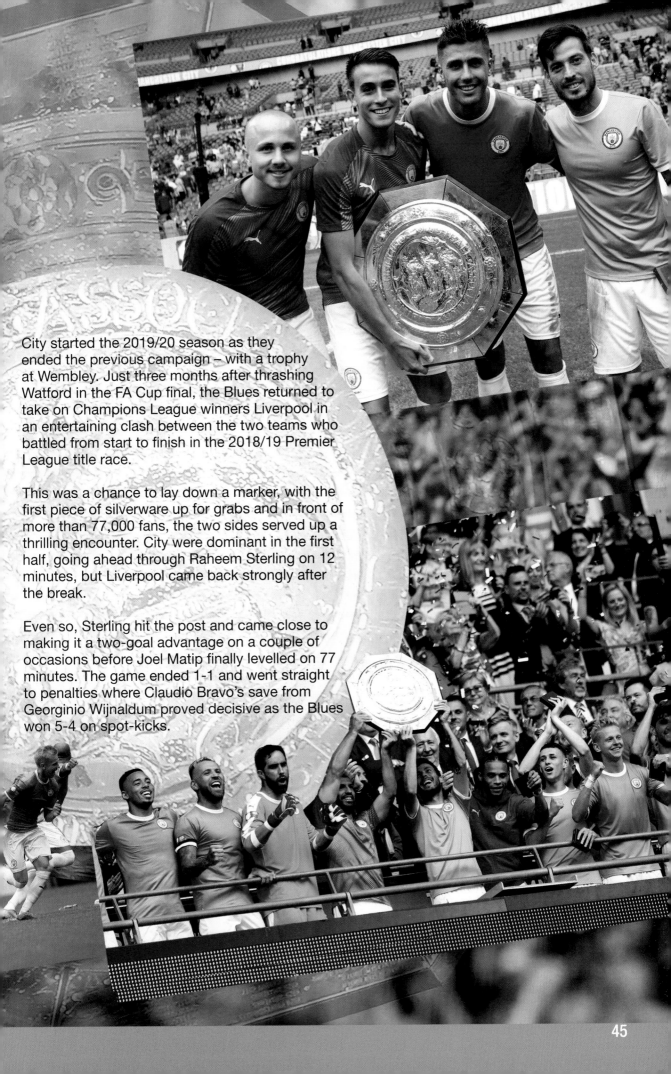

City started the 2019/20 season as they ended the previous campaign – with a trophy at Wembley. Just three months after thrashing Watford in the FA Cup final, the Blues returned to take on Champions League winners Liverpool in an entertaining clash between the two teams who battled from start to finish in the 2018/19 Premier League title race.

This was a chance to lay down a marker, with the first piece of silverware up for grabs and in front of more than 77,000 fans, the two sides served up a thrilling encounter. City were dominant in the first half, going ahead through Raheem Sterling on 12 minutes, but Liverpool came back strongly after the break.

Even so, Sterling hit the post and came close to making it a two-goal advantage on a couple of occasions before Joel Matip finally levelled on 77 minutes. The game ended 1-1 and went straight to penalties where Claudio Bravo's save from Georginio Wijnaldum proved decisive as the Blues won 5-4 on spot-kicks.

SOCIAL MEDIA KINGS

Who are the Manchester City social media kings?

Our players have millions of followers on social media when the numbers are combined, but who are the leaders when it comes to social media popularity? Below are two lists – one for Twitter and one for Instagram – they show the top 10 on each platform with a third list adding both together to find the top five overall…

 Twitter: Top 10

- 13.03M – SERGIO AGUERO
- 3.86M – DAVID SILVA
- 1.98M – CLAUDIO BRAVO
- 1.85M – RAHEEM STERLING
- 1.79M – KEVIN DE BRUYNE
- 1.67M – FERNANDINHO
- 1.59M – RIYAD MAHREZ
- 1.44M – KYLE WALKER
- 1.36M – LEROY SANE
- 1.02M – BENJAMIN MENDY

 Instagram: Top 10

- 12.5M – GABRIEL JESUS
- 11.7M – SERGIO AGUERO
- 8.3M – KEVIN DE BRUYNE
- 5.3M – RAHEEM STERLING
- 4.3M – LEROY SANE
- 2.8M – RIYAD MAHREZ
- 2.8M – BENJAMIN MENDY
- 2.5M – ILKAY GUNDOGAN
- 2.1M – FERNANDINHO
- 1.5M – BERNARDO SILVA

Combined results
Top 5 Social Media Kings

- 25M – SERGIO AGUERO
- 13.36M – GABRIEL JESUS
- 10.09M – KEVIN DE BRUYNE
- 5.66M – LEROY SANE
- 5.06M – DAVID SILVA

*as of 1 July 2019

DAVIDSILVA

EDERSON MORAES

NAME: EDERSON MORAES
POSITION: GOALKEEPER
SQUAD NUMBER: 31

DATE OF BIRTH: 17/08/1993
PREVIOUS CLUBS: RIO AVE, BENFICA

2018/19 APPS (ALL COMPS): 55
2018/19 GOALS (ALL COMPS): 0
TOTAL CITY CAREER:
PLAYED: 100 GOALS: 0

CLAUDIO BRAVO

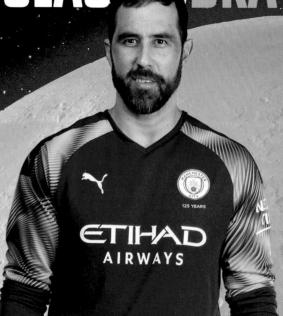

NAME: CLAUDIO BRAVO
POSITION: GOALKEEPER
SQUAD NUMBER: 1

DATE OF BIRTH: 13/04/1983
PREVIOUS CLUBS: COLO COLO, REAL SOCIEDAD, BARCELONA

2018/19 APPS (ALL COMPS): 1
2018/19 GOALS (ALL COMPS): 0
TOTAL CITY CAREER:
PLAYED: 44 GOALS: 0

*correct up to the end of the 2018/19 season

DANIEL GRIMSHAW

NAME: DANIEL GRIMSHAW
POSITION: GOALKEEPER
SQUAD NUMBER: 32

DATE OF BIRTH: 16/01/1998
PREVIOUS CLUBS: ACADEMY

2018/19 APPS (ALL COMPS): 0
2018/19 GOALS (ALL COMPS): 0
TOTAL CITY CAREER: 0
PLAYED: 0 GOALS: 0

ARIJANETMURIC

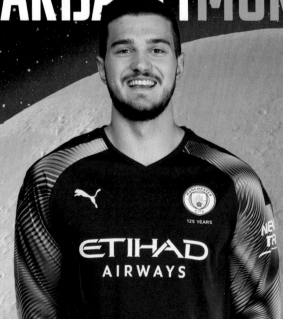

NAME: ARIJANET MURIC
POSITION: GOALKEEPER
SQUAD NUMBER: 49

DATE OF BIRTH: 07/11/1998
PREVIOUS CLUBS: ACADEMY, NAC
BREDA (LOAN)

2018/19 APPS (ALL COMPS): 5
2018/19 GOALS (ALL COMPS): 0
TOTAL CITY CAREER:
PLAYED: 5 GOALS: 0

ON LOAN

BENJAMINMENDY

NAME: BENJAMIN MENDY
POSITION: LEFT-BACK
SQUAD NUMBER: 22

DATE OF BIRTH: 17/07/1994
PREVIOUS CLUBS: LE HAVRE, MARSEILLE, MONACO

2018/19 APPS (ALL COMPS): 14
2018/19 GOALS (ALL COMPS): 0
TOTAL CITY CAREER:
PLAYED: 22 GOALS: 0

KYLEWALKER

NAME: KYLE WALKER
POSITION: RIGHT-BACK
SQUAD NUMBER: 2

DATE OF BIRTH: 28/05/1990
PREVIOUS CLUBS: SHEFFIELD UNITED, NORTHAMPTON (LOAN). SPURS, SHEFFIELD UNITED (LOAN), QPR (LOAN), ASTON VILLA (LOAN)

2018/19 APPS (ALL COMPS): 52
2018/19 GOALS (ALL COMPS): 2
TOTAL CITY CAREER:
PLAYED: 100 GOALS: 2

OLEKSANDR ZINCHENKO

NAME: OLEKSANDR ZINCHENKO
POSITION: MIDFIELDER/FULL-BACK
SQUAD NUMBER: 11

DATE OF BIRTH: 15/12/1996
PREVIOUS CLUBS: UFA, PSV, JONG PSV

2018/19 APPS (ALL COMPS): 29
2018/19 GOALS (ALL COMPS): 1
TOTAL CITY CAREER:
PLAYED: 43 GOALS: 1

JOHN STONES

NAME: JOHN STONES
POSITION: CENTRAL DEFENDER
SQUAD NUMBER: 5

DATE OF BIRTH: 28/05/1994
PREVIOUS CLUBS: BARNSLEY, EVERTON

2018/19 APPS (ALL COMPS): 39
2018/19 GOALS (ALL COMPS): 0
TOTAL CITY CAREER:
PLAYED: 109 GOALS: 5

NICOLASOTAMENDI

NAME: NICOLAS OTAMENDI
POSITION: CENTRAL DEFENDER
SQUAD NUMBER: 30

DATE OF BIRTH: 12/02/1988
PREVIOUS CLUBS: VELEZ SARSFIELD, PORTO, VALENCIA, ATLETICO MINEIRO (LOAN)

2018/19 APPS (ALL COMPS): 33
2018/19 GOALS (ALL COMPS): 1
TOTAL CITY CAREER:
PLAYED: 171 GOALS: 8

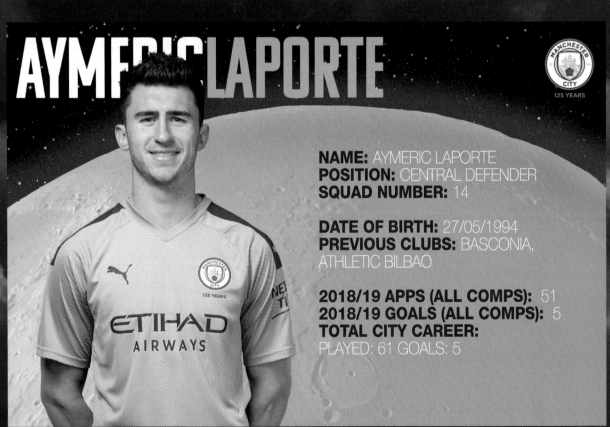

AYMERICLAPORTE

NAME: AYMERIC LAPORTE
POSITION: CENTRAL DEFENDER
SQUAD NUMBER: 14

DATE OF BIRTH: 27/05/1994
PREVIOUS CLUBS: BASCONIA, ATHLETIC BILBAO

2018/19 APPS (ALL COMPS): 51
2018/19 GOALS (ALL COMPS): 5
TOTAL CITY CAREER:
PLAYED: 61 GOALS: 5

FERNANDINHO

NAME: FERNANDINHO
POSITION: DEFENSIVE MIDFIELDER
SQUAD NUMBER: 25

DATE OF BIRTH: 04/05/1985
PREVIOUS CLUBS: ATLETICO PARANAENSE, SHAKHTAR DONETSK

2018/19 APPS (ALL COMPS): 42
2018/19 GOALS (ALL COMPS): 1
TOTAL CITY CAREER:
PLAYED: 273 GOALS: 23

RODRI

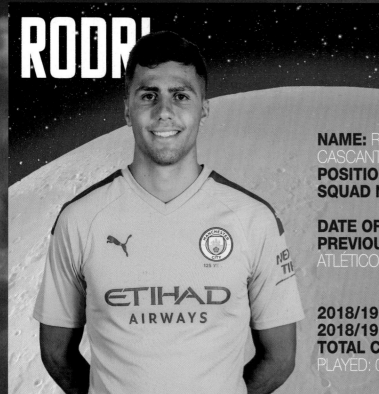

NAME: RODRIGO HERNÁNDEZ CASCANTE
POSITION: DEFENSIVE MIDFIELDER
SQUAD NUMBER: 16

DATE OF BIRTH: 23/06/1996
PREVIOUS CLUBS: VILLARREAL ATLÉTICO MADRID

2018/19 APPS (ALL COMPS): 0
2018/19 GOALS (ALL COMPS): 0
TOTAL CITY CAREER:
PLAYED: 0 GOALS: 0

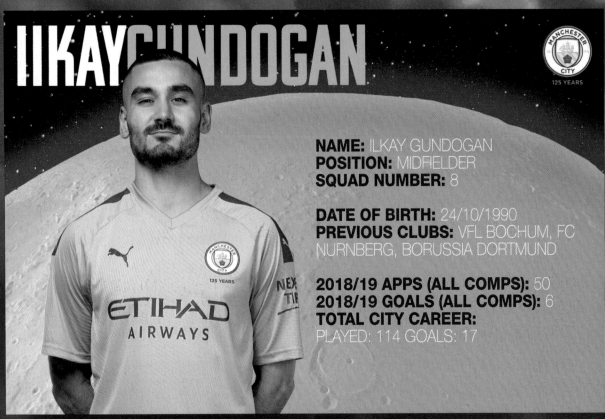

IIKAYGUNDOGAN

NAME: ILKAY GUNDOGAN
POSITION: MIDFIELDER
SQUAD NUMBER: 8

DATE OF BIRTH: 24/10/1990
PREVIOUS CLUBS: VFL BOCHUM, FC NURNBERG, BORUSSIA DORTMUND

2018/19 APPS (ALL COMPS): 50
2018/19 GOALS (ALL COMPS): 6
TOTAL CITY CAREER:
PLAYED: 114 GOALS: 17

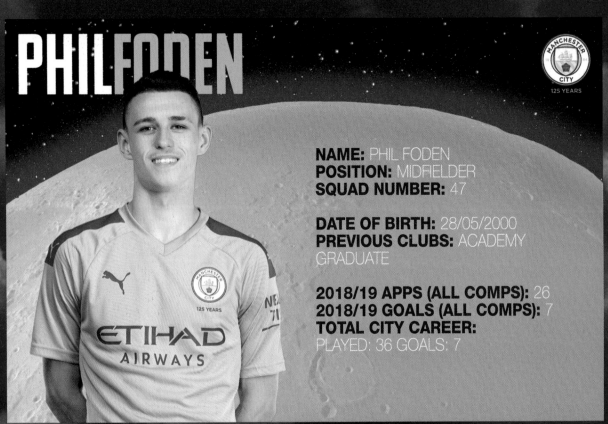

PHILFODEN

NAME: PHIL FODEN
POSITION: MIDFIELDER
SQUAD NUMBER: 47

DATE OF BIRTH: 28/05/2000
PREVIOUS CLUBS: ACADEMY GRADUATE

2018/19 APPS (ALL COMPS): 26
2018/19 GOALS (ALL COMPS): 7
TOTAL CITY CAREER:
PLAYED: 36 GOALS: 7

LEROY SANE

NAME: LEROY SANE
POSITION: WINGER
SQUAD NUMBER: 19

DATE OF BIRTH: 11/01/1996
PREVIOUS CLUBS: SCHALKE 04

2018/19 APPS (ALL COMPS): 47
2018/19 GOALS (ALL COMPS): 16
TOTAL CITY CAREER:
PLAYED: 133 GOALS: 39

DAVID SILVA

NAME: DAVID SILVA
POSITION: ATTACKING MIDFIELDER
SQUAD NUMBER: 21

DATE OF BIRTH: 08/01/1986
PREVIOUS CLUBS: VALENCIA, EIBAR
(LOAN), CELTA VIGO (LOAN)

2018/19 APPS (ALL COMPS): 50
2018/19 GOALS (ALL COMPS): 10
TOTAL CITY CAREER:
PLAYED: 396 GOALS: 71

MANCITY SQUADPROFILES 2019/20

KEVIN DE BRUYNE

NAME: KEVIN DE BRUYNE
POSITION: ATTACKING MIDFIELDER
SQUAD NUMBER: 17

DATE OF BIRTH: 28/06/1991
PREVIOUS CLUBS: GENK, CHELSEA, WERDER BREMEN (LOAN), WOLFSBURG

2018/19 APPS (ALL COMPS): 32
2018/19 GOALS (ALL COMPS): 6
TOTAL CITY CAREER:
PLAYED: 173 GOALS: 41

BERNARDOSILVA

NAME: BERNARDO SILVA
POSITION: ATTACKING MIDFIELDER
SQUAD NUMBER: 20

DATE OF BIRTH: 10/08/1994
PREVIOUS CLUBS: BENFICA, MONACO

2018/19 APPS (ALL COMPS): 47
2018/19 GOALS (ALL COMPS): 13
TOTAL CITY CAREER:
PLAYED: 100 GOALS: 22

RAHEEM STERLING

NAME: RAHEEM STERLING
POSITION: WINGER
SQUAD NUMBER: 7

DATE OF BIRTH: 08/12/1994
PREVIOUS CLUBS: QPR, LIVERPOOL

2018/19 APPS (ALL COMPS): 51
2018/19 GOALS (ALL COMPS): 25
TOTAL CITY CAREER:
PLAYED: 191 GOALS: 69

RIYAD MAHREZ

NAME: RIYAD MAHREZ
POSITION: ATTACKING MIDFIELDER
SQUAD NUMBER: 26

DATE OF BIRTH: 21/02/1991
PREVIOUS CLUBS: QUIMPER, LE
HAVRE II, LE HAVRE, LEICESTER CITY

2018/19 APPS (ALL COMPS): 44
2018/19 GOALS (ALL COMPS): 12
TOTAL CITY CAREER:
PLAYED: 44 GOALS: 12

GABRIEL JESUS

NAME: GABRIEL JESUS
POSITION: STRIKER
SQUAD NUMBER: 33

DATE OF BIRTH: 03/04/1997
PREVIOUS CLUBS: PALMEIRAS

2018/19 APPS (ALL COMPS): 47
2018/19 GOALS (ALL COMPS): 21
TOTAL CITY CAREER:
PLAYED: 100 GOALS: 45

SERGIOAGUERO

NAME: SERGIO AGUERO
POSITION: STRIKER
SQUAD NUMBER: 10

DATE OF BIRTH: 02/06/1988
PREVIOUS CLUBS: INDEPENDIENTE,
ATLETICO MADRID

2018/19 APPS (ALL COMPS): 46
2018/19 GOALS (ALL COMPS): 32
TOTAL CITY CAREER:
PLAYED: 337 GOALS: 231

LEROYSANE

QUIZ AND PUZZLE ANSWERS

GUESS WHO? #1
(From page 14)

01 PHIL FODEN

02 BENJAMIN MENDY

03 DAVID SILVA

04 EDERSON

WORDSEARCH #1
(From page 15)

```
L O Z Y K L N N K T N P
M D I D D K K T K O G A
D R N F K N R Z S G I J
R A C W O D E R M C Z L
M N H A K D E M R J A R
T R E L L D E A R P H T
J E N K E L G N O L S C
N B K E V W F R R V E C
F N O R P P T J F B N K
R K G G K E G L Q K O Q
N S T E R L I N G M T F
V Z E R H A M T B C S G
```

CROSSWORD
(From page 18)

```
                    MOONCHESTER      H        KY
            BENJAMINMENDY            E        LW
        K                   C       B         EA
    K   E           S       L       L   FERNANDINHO
    A   V     S     T   FOURMIDABLES S   AR
    R   I     B     E   A   U        S   LA
    E   N     L     P   R   D            KN
    N   D     U     H   A   E            ED
    B   E  B  R A H E E M S T E R L I N G   R
    A   B  L  A   O   E   I   O      EDERSON
    R   R  U  R   U   L   H   B      R      H
    D   U  E  D   G   R   A   R SERGIOAGUERO
    S   Y  M  S   H   O   D   A      Y
    L   N  O  L   T   Y   S   V      D
    E   E  O  E   O       A   O      M
    Y   BERNARDO  N       N          A
              DAVIDSILVA  E          H
          VINCENTKOMPANY  U          R
                          E          E
                          Z
```

SPOT THE BALL #1 **6E**
(From page 19)

```
1  2  3  4  5  ⑥  7  8
                           A
                           B
                           C
                           D
                           Ⓔ
                           F
                           G
                           H
```

SPOT THE BALL #2 **3D**
(From page 30)

```
1      2      ③      4
                        A
                        B
                        C
                        Ⓓ
```

GUESS WHO? #2 (From page 31)

01 OLEKSANDR ZINCHENKO

02 RAHEEM STERLING

03 AYMERIC LAPORTE

04 GABRIEL JESUS

WORDSEARCH #2 (From page 40)

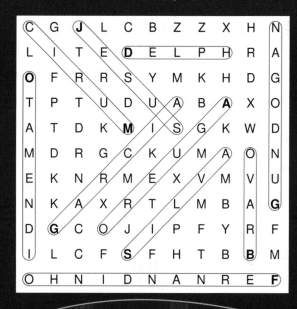

THE *BIG* CITY QUIZ 2019 (From page 26-29)

1. FABIAN DELPH AND NICOLAS OTAMENDI
2. ANDERLECHT
3. CRYSTAL PALACE
4. RAHEEM STERLING
5. SERGIO AGUERO
6. NEWPORT COUNTY
7. TRUE – FERNANDO LLORENTE'S GOAL WAS GIVEN DESPITE APPEARING TO HIT HIS ARM AND GO IN AND RAHEEM STERLING'S LAST-MINUTE GOAL WAS RULED OUT FOR OFFSIDE.
8. SPURS
9. KOSOVO
10. HUDDERSFIELD TOWN
11. RAHEEM STERLING
12. TWO – HOFFENHEIM AND SCHALKE
13. RIYAD MAHREZ
14. AYMERIC LAPORTE
15. B) 10-0
16. A) LISBON
17. EDERSON
18. LYON
19. FOUR
20. C) 5 – SPURS PREMIER LEAGUE, CHELSEA (FA COMMUNITY SHIELD & CARABAO CUP),

BRIGHTON (FA CUP SEMI-FINAL) AND WATFORD (FA CUP FINAL)
21. BURNLEY
22. PHIL FODEN
23. SERGIO AGUERO
24. LEROY SANE
25. LIVERPOOL
26. TWO – CONTINENTAL CUP AND WOMEN'S FA CUP
27. 4-3
28. LEICESTER CITY
29. 18 OF 19 GAMES
30. EIGHT – ONLY LOSSES WERE CHELSEA (PREMIER LEAGUE) AND SPURS (CHAMPIONS LEAGUE)
31. B) NEWCASTLE UNITED
32. BRAHIM DIAZ
33. BURTON ALBION
34. TRUE
35. TRUE – CHELSEA (FA COMMUNITY SHIELD) AND WATFORD (FA CUP FINAL)
36. RIYAD MAHREZ
37. PUMA
38. 17
39. C) GRAN CANARIA
40. ESPANYOL

WHERE'S RAHEEM?
Can you spot Raheem Sterling in the crowd?